WHAT LEGACY WILL YOU LEAVE?

WHAT LEGACY WILL YOU LEAVE?

A Guide to Living a Legacy Conscious Life

The Visionary Library Book 4

By Tony Rogers Jr.

Copyright 2023 by Tony Rogers Jr.
Published by Visionary Press

No portion of this publication may be reproduced, stored in any electronic system or transmitted in any form or by any means, electronic, mechanical, photocopy, recording or otherwise, without written permission from the author. Brief quotations may be used in literary reviews.

Note:
No AI programs were used to generate content in this book or any other of my published works.

Connect with Tony: thevisionarysocietyinfo@gmail.com

DEDICATION

To my son, Tony Rogers III, my aim is to leave a legacy that will make you proud to call me dad.

CONTENTS

Preface 1

CHAPTER 1 – Mortality Motivation 3
    Death – The Ultimate Motivator 4
    A Word from Seneca 6

CHAPTER 2 – Defining Legacy 9
    How I Define Legacy 9
    A Tough (but Necessary) Question 11
    Legacy-Based Decision Making 12

CHAPTER 3 – Mentoring the Next Generation 15
    What Is Mentorship? 16
    The Mentor's Job 17
    The Cycle of Mentorship 22
    The Power of Indirect Mentorship 22

CHAPTER 4 – Writing your Legacy Plan 25
    Legacy Has Layers 26
    My Whole-Life Approach to Legacy Planning 26

Your Eulogy 34
My Mother's Legacy 35
Other Books from the Author 39
About the Author 41

The Visionary Library is an ongoing series of books written specifically for visionaries—common people with an uncommon desire to bring about positive change in the world.

This book is #4 in the series.

PREFACE

Recently, my 39th birthday passed. I had mixed feelings about being celebratory. I truly feel blessed to be alive and I'm immensely appreciative of how far I've come on my journey; however, growing a year older got me thinking about how much life I had left to live. I couldn't help but think, "How much time do I have left to make a difference in this world? How much time do I have left to accomplish all the things I want to achieve?"

In some ways, I felt cursed by my ambitions, intensely pulled in many directions yet void of the necessary margin in life to entertain them. The speed at which progress happens and life dissipates appears to operate on two different scales of time. Maybe all of this is futile.

After processing a barrage of thoughts like this on and off for about a week, I realized it was becoming unproductive. I didn't want to continue in this downward spiral of thinking. I had to remind myself that I couldn't control how much time I had left but *I could control what I did with the time I had*. I decided to stop thinking about myself and what I couldn't do and refocus my efforts on my purpose. I've had the idea to write this book for a little over two years. Finally completing it has been exactly what I needed to shift my perspective. I must say, though, it was tough to write. Not solely from an intellectual perspective, as you might expect, but also from an emotional one.

Being forced to think through and write out my thoughts regarding legacy has been a therapeutic experience. I was already a legacy-conscious person before writing this book, but since finishing it, that perspective has increased fivefold. My hope is that you find as much clarity from reading it as I found in writing it.

Chapter 1
MORTALITY MOTIVATION

"The prospect of death leads to a greater appreciation of life"

— Tom Rath

I recently received a text message from a friend informing me that his father had died the previous day. I responded with my sincere condolences and offered my support. As he described the details of this unfortunate event, it reminded me of the finality of death. We all have a finite amount of time on this earth. Every day, each of us moves closer to that unknown finish line. I don't say this to come off as extreme or morbid. I say this simply because it is an undeniable fact. Everything created has its own birth-death lifecycle. Humans experience this cycle in a unique way compared to other products of nature because we are conscious of it. This awareness puts our species in a position to potentially benefit from this knowledge.

Death – The Ultimate Motivator

You may be thinking, "How can I benefit from knowing I'm going to die?" Having a healthy sense of your mortality can move you toward a more meaningful and fulfilling life in several ways.

1. It can motivate you.

Death is the ultimate motivator. The impermanence of life imbues it with an urgent call to LIVE. We all have different views on what it means to live a full life. For me, truly living doesn't include hedonism or the pursuit of an overly indulgent life for its own sake. Living entails testing the outer limits of my potential, exploring and expressing my unique talents, and doing anything else that aids me in becoming the best version of myself.

In whatever way you define life for yourself, just know the opportunity to experience it won't always be there. If I do my job, this book will become a catalyst to you moving in the direction of living a full life—whatever that means for you.

2. It can change your perception of time.

When you understand that time is a nonrenewable commodity and your life is a reflection of how you choose to allocate that time, the value you place on your time will automatically increase. Anything that you truly value, you will protect, and protection of your time requires learning to set boundaries against outside intruders.

Our hyper-connected, technology-driven society is engineered to attract and keep our attention twenty-four hours a day. A constant flow of requests, advertisements, and notifications will quite literally distract your life away if you allow them to do so. Establishing and enforcing boundaries around your time will ensure you remain in control of your most precious asset.

3. It can affect what you view as important.

Values are individual beliefs about what someone perceives as important. They serve as guiding principles for behavior and decision making. Everyone lives by their own set of values, whether consciously or unconsciously. A person who has a high value on physical health will conduct him or herself differently from someone who does not. Human behavior is eminently resistant to change, but this resistance can shift rather quickly if an internal or external force sparks a change in a person's values. You frequently see this happen after significant life events such as the birth of a child, an alarming health diagnosis, or a religious conversion.

My point is this: coming to terms with the scarcity of life will almost certainly change what you view as important. This transformation could be manifested in drastic or subtle changes in your daily life. For example, a notorious workaholic may suddenly begin declining extra hours at work to spend more quality time with his loved ones.

Essentially, it will show up as new behavior toward anything you tended to neglect or take for granted prior to your newfound appreciation of your mortality.

4. It can spark introspective philosophical inquiry.

A heightened awareness of your mortality may lead you to introspective questions of purpose, meaning, and legacy. Questions such as:

- "What will my legacy be?"
- "How do I want to be remembered?"
- "How can I leave the world better than I entered it?"

If a posthumous biography was written about your life up to this point, what would it say? Would you be proud of your story? My guess is, whether your answer to that last question is yes or no, deep inside you know you have more to give, more story to live. If not, I doubt you would be reading this book. We will revisit these questions in forthcoming chapters.

A Word from Seneca

The suggestion to draw a sense of motivation and urgency from the inevitability of your death is not a new concept. For thousands of years, philosophers, spiritual teachers, and other great thinkers have written about the fleeting nature of life and mankind's resistance to grasping the seriousness of this issue.

The following is some of my favorite commentary on the matter.

> *"You are living as if destined to live forever; your own frailty never occurs to you; you don't notice how much time has already passed but squander it as though you had a full and overflowing supply—though all the while that very day which you are devoting to somebody or something may be your last.*

"Life is long enough, and a sufficiently generous amount has been given to us for the highest achievements if it were all well invested. But when it is wasted in heedless luxury and spent on no good activity, we are forced at last by death's final constraint to realize that it has passed away before we knew it was passing. So it is: we are not given a short life but we make it short, and we are not ill-supplied but wasteful of it."

I came across these passages in a little book titled "On the Shortness of Life" by Seneca, the great Roman philosopher. They hit home for me because I, too, am subject to taking the gift of life for granted. Sometimes I slip into cycles of worry or complaining about petty matters that in the grand scheme of things aren't deserving of my attention at all.

I understand this is normal and simply human nature at work, so I don't beat myself up for it, but I do hold myself accountable for returning to a baseline of gratitude about life no matter what external circumstances present themselves. This small reframing of my thinking usually provides the attitude adjustment I need rather quickly. Doing this is a practical way I show an ongoing recognition of how quickly the end could come. As Seneca mentioned in the above passage, "… that very day which you are devoting to somebody or something may be your last."

CHAPTER 2

DEFINING LEGACY

"Are we being good ancestors?"

– JONAS SALK

For as long as I can remember, I've been intrigued by the idea of legacy. Growing up, I idolized people who appeared to fit my short-sighted view of what legacy meant to me at the time. I thought legacy was directly connected to money and fame; by extension, I assumed it was only something the rich and powerful could attain. I believed you had to achieve a certain level of status in social hierarchy before anything regarding legacy could be bestowed upon you. Thankfully, I've matured in my view and perceive legacy in a different light today.

How I Define Legacy

I define legacy as a person's social influence beyond their physical death. It has to do with how you are remembered in the hearts and minds of people who directly knew you or felt the effects of something you created. For visionaries like you and me, people intent on making a positive difference in the world, this definition has a few important implications to call out.

1. Not all legacies are positive.

A person's social influence can be negative or positive; so, too, can a person's legacy. If I ask you to think of someone you consider to have a negative legacy, I'm sure you wouldn't need to think long before you came up with a name or two. The person may not be around anymore physically, yet the negative effects of their presence still lingers.

An extreme historical example of this would be someone like Adolf Hitler, who was a tyrannical German dictator from the 1930s. He is a well-known historical figure but for many of the wrong reasons. His time in power was a disastrous one. In an effort to see his pro-German and anti-Jewish vision become a reality, he started World War II and began the systematic, mass extermination of all Jews and their allies in an event now known as The Holocaust. His life and legacy are used as a cautionary tale instead of a positive demonstration of what visionary leadership can accomplish. Again, this is an extreme historical example, but I felt using it would best drive the point I'm making home.

A negative legacy is the worst-case scenario for a visionary and the antithesis of everything we work to accomplish. My hope is that none of my readers have this experience and that we only leave behind noble legacies that do good in the world. (Note: a noble legacy does not mean a perfect one. Perfection does not exist in the realm of humans.)

2. Relationships are the foundation of legacy.

Everyone has social influence of some kind; therefore, everyone will leave a legacy. Doing so isn't a choice; it's a byproduct of living in a social system built on an interconnected web of relationships.

Almost every role you play in life is linked to another person. These people are the keepers of your legacy. They hold memories of you, keep photos of you, and pass on stories of what you did and things you accomplished. To prioritize people is to also prioritize legacy because your influence on people is what determines your legacy.

So, as you set out to build your great vision of success, make sure it includes building solid relationships with people. This includes your family, friends, customers, clients, and co-workers. Never forget that the people you touch through your life and your work are what keep your legacy alive. As author and leadership expert John Maxwell says, "I don't know what you want to accomplish in life, but I can tell you this: a legacy lives on in people, not things."

A Tough (but Necessary) Question

Let's revisit a question I proposed in the last chapter.

If your life ended today and your story was released to the public as a depiction of your legacy, would you be proud of it?

If your answer to this question is no, it's probably because there are some things you feel are left undone. Life left unlived. Goals unachieved. Potential unfulfilled.

You can't go back and change anything that happened up to this point, but you can write new chapters in your story moving forward. This process begins with acknowledging where you are currently, then laying any thought of it aside as you focus on the new actions you'll take in line with the future you want to build.

Think of your legacy as an ongoing biographical story written with the ink of your daily decisions and actions. Since you alone are in control of your decisions and actions, you alone are in control of your legacy.

Legacy-Based Decisions

Before we move on to the next chapter, let's talk a bit more about decision making. I want to give you a tool I picked up along my journey that will help you make wise choices as it relates to your legacy. I call it legacy-based decision making.

A legacy-based decision is any decision that will move you in the direction of your desired future legacy. The goal is to make most, if not all, of your decisions from this frame of reference. Using your future legacy as a filter through which to make decisions in the present will dramatically improve the chances of achieving your goal.

I use this when making big or small decisions, and it has served me well. The decision to begin writing books and doing public speaking engagements were both purely legacy-based decisions. Although I do both of these activities fairly often, I find them strenuous, tedious, and anxiety-inducing. Yet I have opted to perform them regardless of what emotional resistance comes up for me because they are required to create the positive social impact I desire to create.

If I choose to let my fear stop me from doing what my legacy requires, I would be living by a fear-based decision instead of a legacy-based decision. That's not a regret I am willing to have at the end of my life.

Like most ideas, this is easy to talk about in theory but can be difficult to apply in practice. We are emotional creatures and, far too often, we prove this by our situational decision making. I can tell you from personal experience that sometimes you will fail to implement this strategy. There is no need to criticize yourself or overthink your behavior. Simply refocus on the goal and get back on track.

Chapter 3
MENTORING THE NEXT GENERATION

"Mentors impact eternity because there is no telling where their influence will stop."

– Jim Dornan

Posterity, not to be confused with prosperity, is the purpose of legacy.

Posterity is defined as:

- Future generations
- A person inheriting and continuing the legacy of a predecessor
- The successors of a person

As visionaries concerned with legacy, we are naturally preoccupied with the success of the next generation. With no one to carry on after your departure, there is no purpose for legacy. In fact, the word legacy gets its meaning by presupposing there is someone to receive what you have to pass down.

Since no one will have a permanent stay on earth, we are only stewards of all that we possess. This includes every leadership position or role we currently hold. A steward is a temporary keeper or guardian of something. As wise stewards, aware of our temporal nature yet highly concerned with posterity, it is only right that we turn our focus towards preparing our successors for their phase of stewardship.

Equipping the next generation to carry on as visionaries in their own right requires mentorship. Mentorship is tough and it can feel thankless, yet mentorship is also honorable and extremely gratifying as you begin to see all the seeds you've planted begin to bear fruit.

What Is Mentorship?

I am a product of mentorship. I owe everything I am currently and everything I will become in the future to mentorship. My hunger to grow—coupled with the generosity and patience of a few key mentors—created the perfect synergistic environment for my mental, physical, and spiritual maturation. I've received a disproportionate amount of reward relative to what I've given to them in return for their generous service. My gratitude for what they did for me is one of the reasons I continue to mentor others today.

Mentorship (or mentoring) refers to the intimate relationship between a mentor and a mentee designed to teach, train, and guide the mentee towards personal or professional growth.

A mentor's job is simple but not easy. It's simple because the essentials can be broken down into four easily understood steps. It's not easy because of how daunting it is to apply them consistently enough, for long enough, with the right situational specific timing, to see the results you and your mentee want and expect from the mentoring relationship. As I've mentioned several times in this book, the theoretical discussion of an idea is easy, yet its realization is always messy and resistant to how you think things should go.

The Mentor's Job – Model, Instruct, Correct, Encourage

1. Model the way.

Modeling the way is the number one job of a mentor. Why? Because who you are speaks before you do. You must first model the way before you have enough credibility to show someone the way. The other steps on this list have no power apart from the credibility that comes from role modeling. The mentorship-mentee dynamic is fundamentally a relationship, and all relationships are built on trust.

Trust is a feeling of security that is organically earned as you prove your trustworthiness over time. Before trust can be established, your mentee wants to know three things:

- Do I want something this person has? (Knowledge, position, lifestyle, inner peace, etc.)
- Does this person's life demonstrate competence in this area?
- Is what I see authentic or false?

Initially, they will gain answers to these questions observationally, meaning they will gather evidence from your outward behavior. If they answer yes, a bridge of trust forms and they become open to the idea of being mentored by you. If they answer no, they will find someone else they regard as a better role model.

It is important to note here that if a mentee of yours ever answers no to any of the questions mentioned above, the relationship is in decline or it is over. This means role modeling is not a one-time event. It is a continuous display of competence, integrity, and self-leadership. The mentee will always be observing you for falsehoods and inconsistencies. Not because they want you to fail but because they want you to succeed. You become the physical embodiment of what success looks like. It gives them something to strive for, something to aspire to.

Becoming a living example of the things you want your mentee to emulate will do more for them than anything you say verbally. Mentorship is leadership. If you can lead *yourself* well, other people will allow you to lead them, too.

2. Instruct for change.

The mentor-mentee relationship has one pivotal goal—transformation. No one takes on a mentor to stay the same. This would be the equivalent of a caterpillar spinning itself into a cocoon in anticipation of becoming a butterfly, only to emerge from the cocoon in its original state. Unlike the caterpillar, who can navigate its metamorphosis alone, your mentee will need outside instruction to effectively maneuver this transformation process.

Years ago, I heard my mentor say, "To teach means to instruct for change." I pulled out my notebook and wrote it down. I like this definition because it reminds us that the goal of teaching is some form of practical change in those being taught, not solely information acquisition.

Sometimes, your mentee will need new information; at other times, they'll need help applying what they already know. Either way, this is where you get to access your most valuable resource—your experience—and shine as the mentor.

What should you teach your mentee? What you teach should be tailored to the needs of your mentees. This is one of the reasons getting to know them on an intimate level is so important. Here are a few things you need to know about your mentees before you can effectively teach them.

- Where are they on their journey?
- How much experience do they have?
- What are their individual goals?
- What are their strengths?
- What are their weaknesses?
- What is their 3–5-year vision for the future?
- How committed are they to doing the work it takes to see results?
- How do they best receive constructive feedback and coaching?

3. Correct in love.

Success never happens in a linear fashion; course corrections are always necessary. If your mentee cannot take constructive criticism well, it will be impossible to mentor them. This flaw in their character will be an impediment to your ability to teach and therefore their ability to grow.

Imagine if Michael Jordan quit every time his coach pulled him aside to correct how he ran a play. No one would remember Michael because he would never have reached the pinnacle of his craft. The most successful people in every field actively seek correction because they know it leads to greatness. Help your mentee understand from the outset that your job as their mentor is to correct errors in their behavior and errors in their thinking. Inform them that correction is an act of love and proof that you believe in their potential to get better. While compiling my notes for this book, I came across a relevant quote on this topic from Dr. Mike Murdock: "When your mentor has stopped correcting you, he has stopped believing in you."

A word of caution regarding correction. There's a stark difference between making necessary corrections for the sake of improvement and being overly critical. An overly critical mentor can cause a host of counterproductive mental health issues for the mentee: performance anxiety, low self-esteem, and perfectionism, to name a few.

A bad mentor can stunt the growth of a mentee by using bad coaching tactics. Being overly critical is certainly one of them.

4. Encourage and affirm.

All mentors work on a spectrum when it comes to administering correction versus encouragement. In my experience, many tend toward one extreme. Either they depend on encouragement and avoid giving correction, or they heavily favor correction and dismiss encouragement as being useful. Both are mistakes. To serve your mentees best, you must learn to do both as needed, regardless of what you have a natural tendency to do.

Remembering to encourage comes down to remembering that relationships are made up of human beings and we all have an emotional need to be encouraged and affirmed. Remembering to give correction comes down to remembering that some behaviors are conducive to our goals while some are not. Behavior that is not must be curbed or it will compound and proliferate.

Since encouragement is not something your followers can go without, it's in your best interest (and theirs) that you understand what it is and how to apply it. I define encouragement as any action that inspires positive change in someone. This can be manifested in many different ways, but I want to focus here on vocal recognition.

By vocal recognition, I mean using verbal or written praise to recognize something intrinsic or extrinsic about someone. This can be done publicly or privately. Intrinsic means something internal to the person. This could mean recognizing a character trait like discipline or hard work. Extrinsic means something external to the person. This could mean recognizing them for hitting a specific financial goal. The rule is this: "Praise what you want repeated." Behaviors that get rewarded are likely to be repeated.

I must admit, I can do better with vocal recognition. Although I have improved considerably over the years, I still find myself failing to outwardly express inwardly felt appreciation more than I would like. I'm not sure how or why I picked up this bad habit, but as a leader, it's unacceptable. Unexpressed appreciation has the same effect as no appreciation from the perspective of the receiver. Until they invent a technology that can read minds, I guess it's something I'll need to keep working on.

The Cycle of Mentorship

As you can see, a mentor has quite a job. It is a simple job, yet certainly not an easy one. But it's well worth the effort. To grasp how important your role is as mentor, you must think about it generationally. Think about it in terms of posterity. The cycle of mentorship works like this:

Receive mentorship —> Give mentorship —> Encourage others to mentor

This cycle begins with anyone who decides to take on the responsibility of mentorship, and ideally, it continues into eternity. Successor after successor. Legacy after legacy.

The Power of Indirect Mentorship

I would be remiss to write a chapter about mentoring without mentioning one of the most influential people in my life. Remnants of his presence can be read in my writing, felt in my public talks, and absorbed through much of my life philosophy.

Dr. Myles Munroe was a Christian pastor based in Nassau, Bahamas. He tragically died, along with eight others in a plane crash, on November 9, 2014. Without him, you would not be reading this book. Without him, the whole trajectory of my life would be different.

I'm mentioning this because of its contextual relevance to our topic. Dr. Munroe's legacy is a real-world example of everything I've said so far in this book. He is proof that, although your physical body will surely perish, your legacy can live on in the people whose lives you touched while you were alive.

I followed Dr. Munroe closely for ten years, but I never met him personally, so how did he have such a profound effect on me?

When you think of mentoring, you probably picture a direct mentoring setup, which is typically one-on-one and in-person. This is the traditional form of mentoring practiced and is something I'll personally continue to engage in as long as I live. There is no substitute for the personal and intimate feel of direct mentoring. Being able to physically watch your mentor in action and absorb the nuances of how they handle different day-to-day situations is unmatched for personal and professional growth.

That said, other viable methods of mentoring have emerged as technological advances such as streaming services, online courses, e-books, and the like have come along. I label anything that fits this category as indirect mentorship. I was introduced to Dr. Myles and many other teachers who have had a significant impact on me because I embraced indirect mentoring.

The cycle of mentorship begins with you receiving mentorship. Never neglect your own personal or professional development. Make a habit of always having some form of mentoring going on in your life, be it direct or indirect. The more you receive, the more your capacity to give will be increased. The best thing you can do for future generations is to become the best version of yourself. The second-best thing you can do is help them do the same.

Become a mentor and encourage others to do the same!

Chapter 4

WRITING YOUR LEGACY PLAN

"Legacies aren't the result of wishful thinking; they're the result of determined doing."

– James Kouzes

Since you've read this far in the book, it's clear that you have an above-average interest in your legacy. Having interest is commendable, but it will quickly diminish and turn to apathy as you return to your daily life. To make things stick long-term and to truly gain practical value from what you've read, you'll need a plan of implementation.

How many people do you think plan their legacy? I think we can agree, many don't think about it at all. If they do, it happens when they perceive themselves as being close to the end of their lives. We know that everyone will leave a legacy of some sort, but very few deliberately decide *what* that legacy will be.

I'm asking you to be the exception. I'm asking you to pre-plan your future legacy NOW and then live based on that plan moving forward.

Legacy Has Layers

Life has many moving parts. It is multi-faceted and multi-layered by nature. The legacy you leave behind will be the same. I have a fear of leaving a one-dimensional legacy. By this, I mean a legacy that has success in one area but falls flat in others. I picked this up from reading biographies of some of my heroes who had success in business or their career but lacked what I would call success in their family life. I say this not to judge that person's journey or come off as unrealistic. I understand that no one can ever create a "perfect" life. My point here is that, for me, that would not be success, so I have specific measures in place to hopefully avoid the same outcome.

This chapter is about building a legacy plan based on what's important to YOU. Your measure of a successful life will be different from mine, and I support that. Success is subjective and based on an individual's goals, family circumstances, work life, and many other factors. I invite you to use my method of legacy planning or completely create your own. The fact that you *create an actual plan* is my primary concern.

My Whole-Life Approach to Legacy Planning

I take a whole-life approach to legacy building and planning. This whole-life approach is built on six pillars of life—six core categories that make up the foundation of my life and contribute to the legacy I want to leave. Separating my life into these arbitrary parts helps me to mentally and conceptually make it more manageable. It also makes ongoing evaluation and execution easier.

Side note – This chapter was particularly tough for me to write because as I ask these questions to you, I am forced to confront my own inadequacies in some of these areas. Although uncomfortable, I welcome this self-reflection. It is further proof that I am still a work in progress, as we all are.

Pillar 1 – Intellectual Legacy

This pillar is about the intellectual ideas that will be a part of your legacy. What ideas or beliefs do you want others to hold as a result of coming in contact with you? Will you leave intellectual property behind as a piece of your legacy? Will you write books or create art?

If you have children, what specific life lessons would you want them to know? What would you most hope to pass on to them? I created a private YouTube channel for each of my children when they were born. I use it to teach them life lessons I think are important. Life is unpredictable, so I did this as a way to preserve my legacy for them in the event that I suddenly pass away for whatever reason. Consider doing this or something similar as well.

_____

_____

_____

_____

_____

_____

_____

_____

_____

_____

_____

_____

Pillar 2 – Relational Legacy

This pillar is about your personal relationships. Good relationships and not so good relationships. How would you rate yourself as a friend? A lover? A father or mother? Can you improve in any way?

(This next question is important) Would the people you're in those relationships with agree with your self assessment? Don't speculate about this; ask them!

Are there any relationships you need to heal? Is there anyone you need to apologize to? Anyone you need to limit contact with or completely dissociate with? Is there anyone you need to spend more time with?

_____

_____

_____

_____

_____

_____

_____

_____

_____

_____

_____

_____

_____

Pillar 3 – Vocational Legacy

This pillar is about your life's work. Are you in your ideal career? If not, what will you do to change that? Do you know your life's purpose? Are you using your inborn gifts and talents to their highest capacity? If not, what will you do to change that?

For more information on this topic, see my book *Visionary: Making a Difference in A World That Needs You.*

_____
_____
_____
_____
_____
_____
_____
_____
_____
_____
_____
_____
_____
_____
_____
_____
_____
_____

Pillar 4 – Financial Legacy

This pillar is about your finances. Do you value financial abundance? Are you where you want to be financially? If not, how will you change this? If you have children, what specific financial habits do you want to pass on to them?

Do you have life insurance? Is your estate planning in order? Have you thought about giving to charity on a regular basis? If not, are you finding other philanthropic ways to help the less fortunate?

_____

_____

_____

_____

_____

_____

_____

_____

_____

_____

_____

_____

_____

_____

_____

_____

Pillar 5 – Spiritual Legacy

This pillar is about your spiritual legacy. For some people, this will be the most important pillar. What are your current spiritual beliefs? Are you content with the level at which your life reflects those beliefs? If not, how will you work to change that?

How has your spirituality benefited you? Do you have a desire to memorialize your spiritual legacy in some way? Maybe through writing a book, composing music, or creating a series of videos?

_____
_____
_____
_____
_____
_____
_____
_____
_____
_____
_____
_____
_____
_____
_____
_____
_____
_____

Pillar 6 – Physical Health Legacy

This pillar is about your physical health and fitness. Is your fitness important to you? Would you want to transfer your current habits about health to the next generation? If not, what will you do to change that?

Once you have a clear understanding of the legacy you want to leave in all six pillars, then the real work can begin. The real work is rearranging your current life in such a way that it matches your new aspirations. This is where the legacy-based decision-making tool from chapter 2 comes in handy.

I typically review my legacy notes monthly to keep my goals and aspirations fresh in my mind. Review your notes as often as you need to remain emotionally connected to your legacy-related goals. It's impossible to live your life based on a plan if you are emotionally disconnected from it.

Your Eulogy

It's possible that you may find using my six pillars method of legacy planning a bit tedious for your liking, so I wanted to leave you with at least one more idea to help you think through your legacy.

Another approach to planning your legacy may be to write your eulogy. A eulogy is a speech paying tribute to the deceased. Doing this exercise can help you get a general idea of what you want your legacy to be. A few prompts to get you started could be:

- What would you want your loved ones to say at your funeral?
- How would you want to be remembered?
- What would you want them to say about who you were as a person?

As you think through these questions and write down the answers, you are simultaneously writing a broad representation of the legacy you should aim to leave upon your death.

My Mother's Legacy

Yesterday morning, after spending quite some time working on this book, I spontaneously asked my mother, "Mom, what do you want your legacy to be? How do you hope to be remembered after you pass on?"

She took a pause and answered, "I would like to be remembered as a loving and kind person. A God-fearing woman. That my children would say I was a good mom. That's most important to me."

I responded, "Well, you certainly succeeded there, Mom. I love you."

WANT TO HELP ME OUT?

Thank you for reading this book. If you received value, please head over to amazon.com and leave a review!

OTHER BOOKS FROM THE AUTHOR

- *Visionary: Making a Difference in a World That Needs You*
- *Writing to Make a Difference: How to Share Your Message and Secure Your Legacy by Writing a Nonfiction Book*
- *The Health-Conscious Leader: Protecting Your Visionary Assignment by Making Health a Priority*
- *Cultivate: 4 Principles to Help Your Mate Recognize and Fulfill Her Potential*
- *The Power of Reading: A Brief Look at the Benefits and Life-Changing Potential of Self-Help Books*
- *Broke: 4 Money Mistakes Keeping You from Financial Freedom and the Life of Your Dreams*
- *Do These Five: 5 Simple Tips for Permanent, Sustainable Weight Loss*
- *Great Like Malcolm: Principles of Greatness from the life of Malcolm X (Coming 2024)*

ABOUT THE AUTHOR

Tony Rogers Jr. is an author, speaker and founder of The Visionary Society - a global training company dedicated to equipping visionaries with the tools and strategies they need to make a difference in the world. He is a proud native of Dayton, Ohio the birthplace of aviation.

Printed in Great Britain
by Amazon